Lyrics of the Soul

Lyrics of the Soul

A collection of spiritual and inspirational poetry; Expressing love, self-encouragement and faith.

Le'Juana Searcy

Writers Club Press
San Jose New York Lincoln Shanghai

Lyrics of the Soul
A collection of spiritual and inspirational poetry;
Expressing love, self-encouragement and faith.

All Rights Reserved © 2000 by Le'Juana Searcy

No part of this book may be reproduced or transmitted in any form or by any means, graphic, electronic, or mechanical, including photocopying, recording, taping, or by any information storage retrieval system, without the permission in writing from the publisher.

Writers Club Press
an imprint of iUniverse.com, Inc.

For information address:
iUniverse.com, Inc.
5220 S 16th, Ste. 200
Lincoln, NE 68512
www.iuniverse.com

ISBN: 0-595-15487-5

Printed in the United States of America

Dedication

My book is a dedication to my mother, the queen of my heart. "Because of your strength, faith in God, and unconditional love—I am blessed beyond eternity."

Contents

Yesterday, Today, Tomorrow 1
I Am Blessed 2
Unconditional Love 3
Creator of Beauty 4
He Knew 5
He Walked 6
Take Time 7
Lord Be Near 8
Faith 9
Gift of Love 10
Love Yourself 11
IF 12
Soul Mate 13
YOU 14
My Everything 15
My Sunshine 16
Because of Your Love 17
Share 18
Because of Love 19
Love Is 20

Sister, Friend	21
Girl Friends	22
Gracious Heart	23
Miracle	24
Diamond	25
My Baby	26
Father	27
Holiday Gift	28
Greatest Joy	29
More Than A Season	30
You Are My Gift	31
Sister Queen	32
Kinfolk Time	33
Sisterly Love	34
Wear Not the Word	35
Maintaining the Crop	37
Friends Are We?	38
Destiny Sealed	39
Sweet Reality	40
One True Friend	41
Alive	42
Way of the Will…	43
Not A race	45
Memory Lane	46
Smell God's Roses	48
Hopeless No More	49
With You	51
Comfort Zone	52
Agenda	53
Friend	54

My Guide	55
Renewed	56
Securely Moored	57
Dancing Love	58
Lessons	59
Repetition	60
Victory	61
Anointed One	62
Thirst Not	63
Ultimate Sacrifice	64
Circle of Love	65
Ribbon of Love	66
Fruit Bowl of Love	67
Loving You	68
Facing Storms	69
Love Remedy	70
Arrival	71
Permanent Place	72
Butterfly	73
My Guiding Light	74
A Piece of Beauty	75
Loving Matrimony	76
God's Design	77
Fruit of My Life	78
Living Miracle	79
Knowing	80
Above Water	81
Mimic	82
Best Day	83
Beautiful Miracle	84

Lyrics of the Soul

Transformation 85
God Bless You 86
Your Love, My Cure 87
Pearl in My Heart 88
My World 89
Solid Ties 90
JESUS 91
My Angel 92
Treasure of Love 93
Multi-Talented 94
Sweet Love 95
Never Say Goodbye 96
Purpose 97
Kiss of Love 98
Rest, God is Listening 99
Soothing 100
Clear View 101
Can't Explain 102
Ingredients 103
Needle and Thread 104
In Motion 105
Spanish Shores 106
Art of A Woman 107
Art of A True Man 108
Speak To Me 109
Reasons 110
Single Mom 111
Perfect Life 113

Acknowledgements

My thanks to my dearest friends for encouraging me to express the voice that God has given to me. "Your support was my pathway." My love to my husband, the jewel in my heart for always being a constant tower of motivation.

Introduction

Love is an unrestrained gift from a divine source of love, a beautiful element giving purpose to our being. As long as there is breath inside of my soul, I will always remain devoted to love, sharing my words in hopes of inspiring others.

Yesterday, Today, Tomorrow

Yesterday, I was a seed lying underneath the dirt.
You walked on me and stomped on me…
I never expressed the hurt.

Today, I am a bud ready to bloom and sprout…
For some strange reason,
You have tried to plow me out.

Tomorrow, I will be a rose with beauty and thorns…
You'll see that I have beauty so deep,
Your heart's jealousy will be torn.

I was strong to overcome your desperate attempt
To brutally destroy me…
But when I'm plucked and placed in a vase,
I'll die in peace and never to you my enemy.

I Am Blessed

In my soul today,
Let Your will lead my way…
I know that You are blessing me every day.
However You bless me,
I am satisfied.
I know that Your love and
Restless eyes will never desert me.
You are my protection.
You have stood in my path to
Shelter me from disaster.
You have sacrificed for me…
Forgiven me out of the bountifulness of Your
Compassionate heart.
You have implemented miracles
Only Your immaculate hands can render.
Lord, with Your love in my life…
I am blessed and I am satisfied.

Unconditional Love

You are never alone.
The Lord will never forsake you.
If you feel discouraged or weak-
Turn to Him.
He is waiting to strengthen
And build you up.
His ears are always open to
Receive your prayers…
He will always embrace you and
Surround your heart with
His unconditional love.

Creator of Beauty

A sunset reflects a luminous glow
Across the sky;
The wind exhales the warmth of its
Tender breath across my skin.
Tranquil waves roar,
Yet quietly they fade…
Leaving shadows embedded
In the warm white sand.
In awe, I observe this display
Of breath taking splendor…
I look over at you-
With affirming knowledge that
God is the creator of beautiful things.

He Knew

The Lord was busy making miracles happen.
One day, He came up with a plan.
This was no ordinary plan,
But a life alternating blessing.
He set His eyes on a specific heart and examined it.
He was very pleased.
He wanted a partner for this heart to
Share unconditional love and happiness.
He drew a path in both directions for
The two hearts to meet...
I still have the map embedded in my heart,
That led me straight to you.
My heart needed a place to go...
He knew.

He Walked

A son was given to us-
So that we would learn to forgive,
Love others, and repent our sins.
Eternal life is ours in return.
Why is it so hard to live life today,
For everlasting life tomorrow?
When you feel life has you defeated-
Don't give up.
Remember the Lord walked for you and I.
With a clear picture of His destination,
Through pain and suffering…
He never turned away-
Never hesitated to die for our salvation.
Willingly He was nailed to the cross,
Sacrificing His life,
So sin would not be our demise.
With open eyes and a clear mind-
We should walk in a direction towards Christ…
Always remembering-
He first walked for you and I.

Take Time

Take time to remember that you are
Not perfect.
Even with flaws,
Love yourself anyway.
Remember to forgive things of the past.
Take time to remember that you are here
For a reason.
Spend more time smiling inside
And reflecting your inner beauty onto others.
Take time to remember that you are
Capable of great things.
Don't feed on words lacking encouragement.
Remember you are one of God's creations.
When others look at you,
They will see God's work…
A true masterpiece.

Lord Be Near

I have a place saved for You
Deep within my heart.
You are a permanent dweller.
I know that I am sheltered
Safe with You near.
You are my vitality…
I breathe because of You.
I love because of You.
Some days may be a challenge,
But I find peace.
I turn to my heart
And find You there-
Waiting patiently,
Warming and strengthening
My spirit…
Carrying on Your enduring promise
To always be right by my side.

Faith

There are mountains waiting to be moved,
Ocean floors without footprints,
And miracles that dance hopelessly around us.

There is Faith…
Mountains are moved,
Seas are parted,
And miracles dance in our lives.

Gift of Love

Faith is knowing that our
Love will endure.
God holds the gift of love.
Let us rekindle the joy
That this gift brings.
Together we will continue
Striving for a solid bond-
Never giving up.
We will make it because our
Love is strong…
Tomorrow awaits a new beginning,
Let's share it together in love.

Love Yourself

You never walk alone.
God is always watching,
Waiting for you to take His hand
And pull Him deep within your heart.
There are miracles waiting to strengthen you-
Giving you the power to love yourself and reflect
The beauty of love onto others.
Every day of your life,
Know that you are loved.
At your most trying times in life-
Remember, you are on someone's mind
Who loves you.
You are His child.
When you reach for Him…
He will comfort you with open arms.

IF

If love grew on trees…
I'd plant a forest,
To watch your love grow
Inside my heart.

If love was the ocean…
I'd surrender to the sea,
To have your love submerge
My whole being.

If love was a song…

I would dance all day,
To ballads in my head
That my love for you play.

If love was the sun…
I would forever glow,
From rays of your love
Burning deep in my soul.

Soul Mate

A phenomenal moment in time…
A rarity in life…
A moving element of fate…

The day you embraced my heart
And became my soul mate.

YOU

You are the beauty in my heart,
The glow in my soul…
Because of you-
I smile brighter,
I laugh longer,
Louder.
Alone I never feel with you…
You are the essence of my joy.

My Everything

When you smile at me,
Your smile flows from your lips
Onto mine-
Radiating my face.
When you are holding me close-
Your arms are comfort and tranquillity,
Wrapping me in warmth.
Your presence is my sweet anticipation;
Near or far…
Your voice is peace that sings in my ear.
Your love is life inside of my heart.
You are and always will be
My everything.

My Sunshine

You are the exuberance
Inside of my heart.
Every moment of the day
You keep a smile
Fixed on my face-
I look forward to
Your voice,
Your touch,
And your love…
Every day you bring to my soul
A love that is filled with sunshine.

Because of Your Love

Your love
Is the sustenance
In my life.
You nourish my heart with sweet,
Tender love…
Loving you is easy.
You bring me serenity and a love that
Is genuine and real.
The splendor of love flows freely
From within my soul every day,
Because I have your love
Sharing my heart's affection.

Share

Share your laughter with me-
It warms my spirit
When it tap dance in my heart.

Share your words with me-
Your knowledge awakens every corner
Of my mind.

Share your heart with me-
Your unconditional love breathes
Warmth into my soul.

Share you with me-
A beautiful piece
Of art,
Designed just for my heart
To love endlessly…

Because of Love

When that special someone is in
Your life,
The definition of true love is revealed.
You know why you have a heart and a soul-
Because God has blessed you
With that person to share
The rest of your life with.
You know why comfort is so important,
Because in each other's arms
Is where you will find it.
You know why understanding is paramount,
Because you love each other
Without judgment.
You know why you feel complete-
You have a partner to share your dreams,
Your future,
And the most beautiful element of life…
Your enduring love for one another.

Love Is

Love is your heart fulfilled because you have
Someone special to complete you.
Someone who listens to you with an open mind,
Smiles at you and fills your soul with joy.
Love is strength through trying times…
Hand and hand
You will conquer challenges.
Love is the freedom to express who you are
And be loved just the same.
Love is a constant sentiment ever growing-
A reoccurring blessing.
Love shines when you look
At the one you love with enlightenment;
You are aware of the gift that united your
Hearts for an eternity.
Love is, because you have one another
To love and cherish for the rest of your lives.

Sister, Friend

You are the definition of true friendship.
You are always there for me.
Bringing a smile to my face,
Racing laughter into my heart.

Your ears never tire…
Your shoulder never weakens
Underneath my head.

You are my sister…
The vitality of my heart.
My Friend…
Joy dancing inside of my spirit.

Girl Friends

We share so much.
It's nice to know that
I can cry, laugh,
Get mad, and still have
The best part of me
By my side.
You are my strength,
My smile, and my
Joy.
Thank you for being my
Best friend.

Gracious Heart

The beauty of giving
Is to give from the heart-
The most precious gift of friendship…
I thank you for this gift,
For it is my most cherished possession.

Miracle

Mother, you are beautiful
Because you are you.
My beloved soothing soul.
You are silent strength that
Uplifts, yet embrace
With such tenderness.
You are a priceless jewel…
A treasured miracle
From heaven.
I thank God
For your sweet rootlet of love…
It ties our bond together for life.

Diamond

Your first smile was the most angelic
Expression that my eyes have ever seen.
I loved you from the first moment
I heard your heart beat...
Once the miracle growing inside of me,
Now you are a blessing for all to see.
I will always love you.
You are the diamond inside of my heart...
Rare, priceless, and beautiful.

My Baby

Because you are a tender soul,
I will embrace you and
Wipe your tears away.
Protect you-
Caress your face with loving kisses.
You will always have a cozy home
Inside of my arms.
You are a blessing from above-
An angel that will be filled with more love
Than your little wings can handle…
Although you will mature and be on your
Own some day,
In my heart you will forever be my baby.

Father

For always being there, I thank you.
Always loving me and lending your ear.
Trusting my judgment you let me be my own person.
Hugs and kisses are precious gifts from your heart…
Everything a daughter treasures about her father you are.
Respecting you comes naturally…especially loving you.

Holiday Gift

There is a gentle radiance
That shines deep within
My heart…
A beautiful gift of
Your enduring love.
It opens my soul
To a joyful celebration of
Everlasting happiness…
This holiday season
And every day
Of the year.

Greatest Joy

Waking up every morning-
Not just on Christmas day,
Or any other holiday
Brings forth a blessing.
A new anticipation to look
Forward to.
God is there waiting for me,
Making sure I have the most
Enjoyment of all in my life…
My family and their love.

More Than A Season

The best feeling in the world
Is assurance that you have someone
In your life;
Not for a season…
But for an eternity.
Friends may come and go.
Blessings like you remain.
You are a gift from God.
I am thankful for the stable
Love you bring to my life.
You are the essence of what a partner
Should be…
You are the reason my heart is fulfilled
And my soul has a mate.

You Are My Gift

You are my gift…
I will always wrap you in
My everlasting love.
Having you in my life
Unfolds the magic of Christmas.
I am blessed with a heart full
Of presents…
Your love is my favorite one of all times.

Sister Queen

Your inspiration is a light
That shines on dark tunnels.
Because of you,
I have an offering greater than all material gains…
Faith and the power
To climb above my dreams.
Your genuine support from the heart
Is a gift from God.
I thank you for your encouragement,
Your honesty,
And your motivating words…
You are a sister that deserves to be
Called a queen.

Kinfolk Time

We are always finding an excuse
To get together.
On holidays or weekends-
It doesn't matter.
We made a commitment to share
A link,
To water the crop of our family tree.
Standing strong to weather many storms,
Our love will never be forlorn.
Spirited stories or the need to unwind-
Brings our family together for kinfolk time.
No matter what day,
No matter the occasion-
Comfort for the soul is a home with elation.

Sisterly Love

I am overjoyed with each espial
Of how amazing God is…
Out of all the people in the world-
He chose us to grow together,
Bonding us with fixed roots.
I am so thankful for His knowledge.
He knew I would need a friend for life…
He created us as sisters
And blessed us to be the best of friends.

Wear Not the Word

Black Coffee, no cream the color of her skin.
I stare and wonder what life is like in her shoes for a day.
Happy she looks with her big afro,
Full lips and curvy figure.
Wonder if is she got called names growing up…
Probably never heard the same names I heard.
All different ones of course, but one…
The one that starts with an N.
No, not nice or Nubian queen.
But you know? That hateful belligerent word
That slithers up the spine like a poisonous
Snake and sinks it's venom deep within the skin.
For no reason other than-
You are with color, different, a curious thing.
Not to be loved, trusted, smiled at, talked to, or respected…
That's what bigots would say.
I could be caramel brown, you could be mocha,
Chocolate or vanilla with a hint of brown sugar…
It doesn't matter.

Because, although I may not have walked in
Her shoes, your shoes, or another sister's shoes…
Someone has judged us both and called
Us that word in their minds, in their hearts…
Knowing the negative history of the word-
Why would one take off their shoes and wear others?
Calling God's creations the same word in casual conversation…
No, I may not know the beautiful sister with the dark skin and afro.
But I see her shoes and they are her own.
Scuffed and tired they may be, but she stands proudly in them.
She wears her color…
By no means does she wear or carry *the word*.

Maintaining the Crop

I am grateful that God is the gardener
Maintaining our family tree.
He is the provider of peace
Running deep within the soil.
He is always preparing a stronger foundation,
And working to enrich the very stem
That carries love into our souls.
Our family is a reflection of unity
And strength…
Because God maintains the crop
That bonds us all together.

Friends Are We?

Can we be friends?
Really get to know one another pass
Fears and illusions?
When you cry and I cry-
Aren't tears still wet when they fall?
Slice open the skin-
Does blood reflect a color
Other than red?
Can we be friends?
Really get to know one another pass
Media or what others portray?
When you smile or I smile, are not
Expressions both joyful illustrations?
Loose something you love,
Does your painful feelings
Reflect emotions other than agony?
Can we be friends?
And see one another for the very first time,
Through our *own* eyes…
As friends?

Destiny Sealed

The sweet sound of your voice
Is warm honey running deep into my soul.
When you whisper I love you,
My heart is bathed in tender delight.
You are my vast journey
To happiness…
Wherever our hearts take us,
We will always discover the joyance
Of our love waiting before us.

Sweet Reality

I could never imagine
In my most vivid dreams,
A love this
Fulfilling and strong…
You show me how amazing dreams really are.
You are a dream come true.
The answer to my prayers.
The love we share is beyond dreams…
It is a truth that God is listening.
He knows when to end the dream,
And bring forth the reality of sweet eternal love.

One True Friend

"Some day you will understand that I am your one true friend."

I never understood what you meant by that.
I always felt I had true friends…
Now I know.
When others turned their backs on me,
You embraced me with open arms.
When the world seemed cold and empty,
You covered me with a warm
Blanket of your love.
When I needed someone to ease the pain,
Your non-judgmental heart was there to heal my wounds.
You have been the sweet in my life turning
My tears of sorrow into
Tears of pure merriment.
I can never thank God enough for blessing my
Life with you as my mother…
I can never thank you enough for being my one true friend.

Alive

I will not live as if I have closed the curtains on life.
I will always embrace the beauty of the sun setting in the sky.
A mild rainy day will remain a soothing potion for my soul.
I will be intrigued by love;
Even when my days are old.
All of the precious things I will not let pass me by.
I will stop and marvel at the elegance of a butterfly.
I will feel the shimmering magic of a star filled night.
If a rose deserves attention for its sweet redolence alone,
Life deserves a happy ending way before it's gone.
Therefore I know,
Alive I am.
Therefore I will show-
Alive I will live.

Way of the Will…

Lash after lash
Until flesh is ripped raw.
Too weak to stand,
Too proud to fall.
Numbed with pain-
Cotton picked hands crack and split.
Still holding on…
Refusing to quit.
Nameless children taken and sold away.
Too young to understand
That they too will breed slaves.
Knowledge forbidden-
But power is in the mind.
Hope was their future-
The weapon against time.
Lash after lash…
Until flesh is ripped raw.
Too weak to stand,
Too proud to fall.

Lyrics of the Soul

I will never forget their
Blood and sweat in the fields,
And how their faith led a way
For me to carry the will.

Not A race

I will not covet your things.
You show off your assets like a snake
With new skin-
I will not marvel or praise you like a king.
I am and always will be blessed abundantly.
I will not feel deprived -
I do not spend my last dime for others
To widen their eyes, at material
Gains I have obtained.
There are no jealous strains…
For I know, it is not vital to surpass my neighbor-
But vitality lies in obtaining a heart to
Please my personal savior.

Memory Lane

Mama was my favorite beautician.
Quality time we shared
With each hair fixing.
Summer was my favorite time.
Everyone played tag, jacks,
Or *Mother May I*.
When we played house,
The boys we didn't miss-
We were proud single moms to
Our many doll kids.
Times when it didn't matter what race or color-
Just innocent play with appreciation for one another…
A day when neighbors were family
Looking out for us.
Quick to set us straight
If we misbehaved or fussed.
Water fights and riding bikes went
Hand and hand.

Le'Juana Searcy

We dropped everything when we heard
Music from the ice-cream man!
Just a black girl child walking down
Memory lane…
Where genuine fun and imagination
Created the games.
A grown up kid wishing life
Was simple again…
When you shared a twin popsicle and
Made a best friend.

Smell God's Roses

You sit in your jag.
Smoking a sweet cigar at the red light.
You never notice hunger around you,
Or others who'd love to eat the crumbs
From your table…
Caviar and galas-
Drinking the finest wine,
Sharing stories with the elite-
Never wondering a day
What you will eat…
Private jets to take you abroad is
A phone call away.
Nose turned up towards people that are not the same.
Just your face in your social mirror
And others of the same plastic material.
Who am I that look upon your crass style?
Without the slightest bit of envy,
Only pity?
I am a free soul that smelled God's roses…
The ones you forgot so long ago,
Grew outside of your perfect window.

Hopeless No More

The usual stale liquor on his breath
As he greets her in the evening.
She feels the sting of his stiff slap-
Way before his hand touches her cheek,
Another normal routine.
She hears the rip in her
Dress as she struggles from his grip…
Funny how he said it looked so pretty on her earlier.
Now it was torn at the shoulder-
Fit for the trash man's pickup.
A hopeful candle flickers on the table-
Next to two untouched plates of
Steak, potatoes, and broccoli…
Tossed salad has gone soggy-
Wine is warm and flat.
Another man is home now.
Not the same one that sat down to breakfast,
Placing a feathery kiss on her lips…
It's the man that kissed the glass of poison too long,
Seduced his habit-
For the last time he'd promise…

Lyrics of the Soul

She's tired of the abuse and worn.
The person she once was left a long time ago-
Through God's help she will reclaim her again.
This time tomorrow she will be gone for good…
The candle and the memory of the battered woman will remain.
Next to the abandoned dinner…
Waiting hopelessly for his same old apology-
And her same old camouflaged smile.

With You

Without you to love-
I am a rose with no sweet air of distinction,
A sun without the bright blue sky to enhance me,
A heart full of love without a single beat,
A laugh without the beaming spirited smile…
With you-
I am a rose in the sun,
Dancing to my favorite beat of love,
While dipped in radiance and laughter.

Comfort Zone

———— ∞ ————

Comfort is contentment within
Your being-
Knowing who you are
Without the definition of someone else.
It is a sense of control-
You are in charge of your
State of mind and destiny…
It is a silent peace within your soul
Because you are free to be you-
You don't desire company to make
You feel connected.
When you are alone, you are accompanied
Only by the best…
Your individuality and inner self love.

Agenda

Lord, You are on the top of my list.
Giving You praise is
My first priority.
Without Your mercy,
Forgiveness,
And sweet loving spirit…

I would never make it through the day.
No matter what life throws my way,
You are always first on my agenda…

Friend

A friend is someone who knows when to comfort…
Someone who is honest even if it hurts-
A friend knows when to talk and when to listen.
Always boosting your ego and easing your tension.
A friend will take your secrets to the grave,
Never sharing them with others or misusing your name.
A friend will be by your side if ever you are ill.
Lifting you back to health-
With love your soul can feel.
A friend will encourage you to be the best you can be.
Recognizing your accomplishments without the least bit of envy.
A friend will never hang mistakes over your head,
Allowing you to learn on your own-
Finding freedom instead.
A friend will walk across coals and swim the widest sea.
In return for the best of both worlds-
Everlasting friendship and their integrity…
I thank you for being that friend to me.

My Guide

I will fall to my knees
Holding my broken spirit.
When I rise,
I will be restored and whole again.
I know the best is yet to come,
You are my survival plan…
I am grateful for Your loving grace.
In You I will always store my faith.
Wherever You lead,
There is a guarantee that spiritual peace will follow.

Renewed

Lord, only You can refresh my soul
And give me continuous peace…
When I think of Your goodness
And tender heart-
I am renewed.
When I look around and see
All of the blessings in my life-
I am renewed.
I am blessed to have
Your extended hand to
Pull me up and renew my spirit
Over and over again…

Securely Moored

As I pass through the waters,
I shall never forget
You will be there with me.
When I feel lost and unstable,
I will cling to my faith
Because You will show me the path of life.
When I am down in spirit, alone, and confused-
I know that You will never forsake me.
I will always remember that You are at my right hand…
I will never be shaken.
You are always faithful.
Your love is the root of my life,
Always there to harvest peace into my soul…
Lord, with Your eyes guarding my life,
My soul will never be broken.

Dancing Love

Your love is enchanting.
It embraces my heart with the melody of love,
My soul flows to the rhythm of blissfulness.
Never before has anyone moved me the way that you do.
At times my mind is a sonata filled with breath
Taking music…
I smile deep inside,
As my heart moves to the beat of
Loving you forever.

Lessons

I have learned to say I'm sorry,
Because it frees the mind from
Bottled pain.
I have learned to say I love you;
Because the chance may never come again.
I have learned happiness starts with me-
Seeking it elsewhere is false reality.
I have learned to walk alone.
Depending on myself has made me strong.
I have learned not to blame.
Taking responsibility allows room for change.
I have learned to invest time in peace.
A sound mind sets you free.
I have learned to envy no one.
I appreciate the person I am-
And what I have to grown on.
I have learned not to sacrifice the truth-
It blends my character with virtue.
I have learned to share joy that I've found,
Carry a heart that is mild,
While making God proud.

Repetition

Your love creates a beautiful glow
That burns deep within me.
Every time I smile to myself,
I think of the extraordinary love
That we share.
Every time I close my eyes
And think of you,
I can't help but fall deep in love…
Over and over again.

Victory

The Lord will fight your battle-
Just give Him your faith.
In return, He will strengthen you
To do all things.
No weapon will form against you.
His shield will turn your enemies around.
No longer will fear entrap your mind…
You are standing on solid ground.
Triumph will lead your spirit to joy
And cast your fears away.
The Lord is your undefeated armor,
He will never leave you astray.

Anointed One

God has unfolded your purpose to us
Through your ultimate sacrifices
And examples-
You have shown others how
To renew their hearts,
Forgive, and live sanctified lives.

Without your knowledge and guidance;
Souls would be lost.

You are an anointed blessing…
A vessel of honor
That links our hearts and souls
To Christ forever.

Thirst Not

Sometimes I need a drink of knowledge.
To help me to understand-
Your love will never forsake me.
You are my father and my friend.

Just one swallow of faith and
I will have the power to reach You.
At times my mouth is dry.
I can not taste the flavor of truth.

I reach for my cup and
You pour Your spirit in,
My thirst is quenched,
My soul is cleansed…
Lord, with You as my supplier-
I shall never thirst again.

Ultimate Sacrifice

As the pain ripped through Your body-
You stayed on the cross.
Without Your sacrifice Lord,
My soul would be lost.

Not once did You contemplate removing
Yourself from the pain.
That is why I love You and
Magnify Your holy name.
You showed me the measure of Your love-
You died for me…
You shed Your precious blood
And gave me eyes to see.
You are my personal savior
In You I will always believe,
You made the ultimate sacrifice
For my soul to be free.

Circle of Love

A continuous structure of love-
No beginning,
No end.
Around at times of trouble;
A pillar of strength…
My band of love for you
Will never come undone.
Through ups and downs-
It remains to spin
Round and round.
Just when you are searching
For the hope in your day-
You can always count on me
To chase your blues away.
Whether it is to pray with you
To the heavens above,
My heart holds a home for you
In the circle of my love.

Ribbon of Love

Without a question-
My love for you will continue to grow
And emerge into something beautiful.
You have defined for me what trust and
Friendship really means.
Our love and respect for one another,
Is a walk on clouds beyond my dreams.
Your love is a gentle ribbon that leaves my heart aglow…
Your perfect way of loving me ties it into a bow.

Fruit Bowl of Love

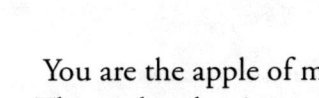

You are the apple of my eye,
The cool melon in my mood,
The bright lemon sunshine in my day,
The soft fuzzy peach in my heart.
I would go bananas without your love…
You are my pineapple orange slice of joy.

Loving You

No one moves me like you do.
I watch you when you aren't
Looking and I blush inside.
You are incredible and I love
You more each day.
I love how you give attention
To everything I say.
I love the smell of your cologne,
The sound of your voice…
I love having a crush on you,
Although we have been married for many years.
I love everything about love…
Especially your tender way of loving me.

Facing Storms

The Lord removed us from the storm,
And our love is in a safe place.
I knew the strife would pass us by-
In Him we stored our faith.
If dark clouds creep in and threaten to tear us apart…
Let's put God before the storm,
To shelter the love in our hearts.

Love Remedy

Sometimes we frame the pain in our lives.
Let's heal our love-
Create new memories,
Share a burst of laughter from solid happiness;
Forgetting about the pain of yesterday.
Let's heal our love with the medicine
God gave us for our souls…
Our love for one another.

Arrival

You walked down a path
That turned into destination.
Challenges and rewards

Shared the same road,
Your hard work and ambition
Brought you to success.

Continue to travel on faith
And believe in yourself-

You will always stand proud on
Ground of many great achievements.

Permanent Place

Every day with you is sunny side up.
I have a blessed combination of
Miracles and contentment in my life.
I know this feeling will surpass
The test of time…
Our love was born
In a permanent place,
Created by God
Called forever…

Butterfly

Someone looked at me-
Never knowing what I would be,
Or that beauty would soar from my wings…
Never knew that I was a gentle and free spirit-
Bringing joy to the eye with my presence.
Vivid and alive I feel.
The tender breeze carries my essence.
I glow with such radiance.
Departed from my mind are the
Days when I crawled
Around feeling drab.
I was brought to light
From my cocoon;
Leaving divine wonder for all to see
And capture in the mind-
What confidence and freedom really feels like.

My Guiding Light

Your love is sweet to my soul,
Medicine to my heart,
And health to my bones.
You are my tower-
Protecting and keeping me safe.
You are my deliverer…
When I close my eyes
And envision Your stripes;
The ones You bared to save my life-
I know Your love for me is
The power in which I exist.
You are my guiding light…
Shining on my soul and
Leading the way to
Your devoted arms forever.

A Piece of Beauty

The Lord gave me a piece of beauty…
The day I saw your smile,
Felt your embrace,
Heard your soothing voice,
Witnessed your strength and ambition.
You turned my tears of sorrow into
Dancing rain in the sunshine.
The Lord gave me a piece of beauty
To carry within the core of
My heart…
It releases its magic
Every time I see your loving face.

Loving Matrimony

God breathed the beauty of love
Into our souls…
He gave us one another to comfort and hold.
He gave us patience and
Communication to talk things through.

He gave us laughter
To share…
And a gentle heart to
Soothe.

God gave us a bond to share for
The rest of our lives…
A foundation of true love
As husband and wife.

God's Design

Love is the structure that holds roots
Of love called family…
A home in the heart that welcomes
You at all times.

Our ground is stronger than steel.
It will never crumble-
Even through storms that
Pass between us…

Whole and firm we stand
Because God is our architect…
He designed our family with love in the floor plan.

Fruit of My Life

You are the fruit that nourishes my body.
Your love is the powerful nutrient
That keeps my heart and mind healthy.
Your blessings are vitamins that
Run through my veins and draw
Strong testaments from my mouth.
Lord, You are the fruit in my life-
You are always in season…
I will always have a hunger for the food
You provide for my soul.
With Your love…
I will never go hungry.

Living Miracle

Every breath is a miracle.
Life into my lungs provided only by You.
What would I do without You?
Every time I inhale and exhale,
I am alive!
You are behind the motion.
You provide the constant repetition.
I will never breath on my own.
Lord, because of Your will
My life is promised…
I thank You for providing me with
The miracle that carries my life to another day.

Knowing

When I awake
You are by my side-
When I fall asleep…
I wake up with you next to me.
I feel a sense of peace
And comfort when I am in your arms.
I think of you throughout
The day and I smile to myself…
I know God had a very beautiful
Plan waiting for me the day I found you.
Your love is the gift God
Gently placed in my heart,
Elating me all the more-
Every time it beats.

Above Water

Don't drown in troubles of yesterday.
When you feel as if your boat is sinking,
Float on your faith.
The Lord is your coast guard.
He will carry you to a peaceful shore.
He will free your heart from the ocean floor.
The Lord will always keep your head above water.
He is your life preserver…
Your soul provider,
He will revive your spirit and make you a survivor.

Mimic

When you smile-
I smile.

You cry-
I cry.

I learn by watching you…

When you scream and shout-
You teach me to do the same things that you do.

Be careful how you mold me.
Teach me what is right…

I am your little mimic-

The child that you gave life.

Best Day

Loving you is easy.
It is natural.
Love is showered
Into my soul endlessly-
Because I have you in my life.
I am whole.
I am content.
No matter what the day brings…
The best part of it is
Having you to come home to.

Beautiful Miracle

I thank God for everything because
I know that I am blessed.
I thank God for the beautiful things;
Especially miracles…
Because without either,
I would not have you.

Transformation

There is something special about silent rain,
Soft tranquil breezes on a warm summer day.
There is an unspeakable gift when a beautiful
Blue sky is the start of your morning,
Or a fresh sheet of white snow
Marks the ground for winter…
It is God's way of showing us that change is good.

God Bless You

Good luck is what you wish someone
When the destination is uncertain…
Yours is very clear.
God is your guide…
As long as the Lord is the shepherd of your way-
You will always be walking on blessed pavement.

Your Love, My Cure

When I was sick-
You brought me soup,
Waited on my hand and foot…
You cured me with your love.
When I fell down and skinned my knee-
You patched me up and wiped my tears,
You cured me with your love.
Your warm words soothed me.
Your strength encouraged me.
Your laughter brightened my day…
Your love will forever remain
The cure all for my heart.

Pearl in My Heart

You are my confidant.
We have shared laughter and created
Memories that we will cherish forever.
You understand me like no one ever will.
My inner most secrets are kept sacred with you.
We have a way of freezing the world
When we are together.
All we notice is the fun that we are having
And the joy of one another's company…
Thank you for being my best friend-
The rock on my shore,
And the pearl in my heart.

My World

I would give you the world
If I could.
Nothing makes me feel better than
Hearing you say
You love me…
Especially when I need it most.
You seem to know just when
My heart is weak and is yearning for strength.
You say those three words to me-
And I am revived again.
The best part of my heart is having
You as my mother…
The best part of my world
Is having you to share it with.

Solid Ties

My heart and friendship is where you will
Always find a home.
Although I may not be there,
God is everywhere.
Through Him love travels.
I am thankful for our solid ties,
It is a blessing to have you in my life.
Always remember in your time of need,
My love is your stone…
Always remaining solid and strong.

JESUS

He lived for you.
Died for you.
Bled for you.
Forgiven you.
Blessed you while you slept,
Walked with you throughout the day.
Wrapped His loving arms around you…
Drinking the sorrow from your tears,
Restored and saved your soul.
His name is Jesus…
His love and mercy is everlasting.

My Angel

You are a gift that continues to unfold in my life.
You have a way of soothing a broken spirit
With your smile.
I could never capture in words the joy I feel to
Have you in my life.
The lessons that you have taught me
Has given me the tools to love
And understand others;
As well as myself.
You have always been a tower of strength
And a soul provider for our family;
For all who have crossed your path…
Not only are you a friend that engraves my
Heart with your love-
You are an angel that has made heaven proud.

Treasure of Love

Nothing fulfills my soul more
Than loving you.
Every day is a new beginning.
You give me such an awakening of
Love, trust, and friendship.
You are the harmony and joy in my life…
Every moment with you is a realization
Of how rich I am in love…
The value of what you have given to my heart is
A wealth of priceless treasure.

Multi-Talented

You were a cook…
You always made the finest food from scratch.
You were a nurse…
You healed me with your tender love and care.
You were a teacher…
You installed in me the lessons of life.
You were a mind reader…
You could always tell when something was bothering me.
You were a magician…
You always made a dollar multiply and go a long way.
You were a counselor…
You always gave advice straight from the heart.
You are my mother…
Eternal love residing deep in my soul.
You are my companion-
Always there to make my world beautiful.

Sweet Love

My heart is dipped in my favorite flavor.
A sweet sugary coated glaze
Called your love.
One thought of you makes me
Beam all over.
I walk with a dance behind every step.
I wear my rose colored glasses every day.
I am in love…
Every moment spent with you
Gives a new meaning to paradise.

Never Say Goodbye

I will never let you out of my heart.
Even though I see your
Smiling face only in my dreams…
The memory of you is alive only in my imagination.
Goodbye means
You are gone for good.
So, instead I will say see you later…
Save me a seat in heaven next to you.
When I get there, I will pick up loving
You from where we left off.

Purpose

Having a voice to express wisdom and love.
Exchanging a smile that makes a stranger's day.
Hugging someone that missed what caring feels like.
Listening to a friend until their pain is gone.
Forgiving others without holding on to the memory.
Encouraging faith to the down in spirit.
Loving from the core of the heart with no regrets.

Kiss of Love

I have found the right person
To love in you….
No one has ever given me love
So exciting and beautiful before.
I am vibrant;
Yet fragile at the same time.
My heart was in need of a precious blessing.
That is why God placed it
In the palm of your hands…
And you kissed it with your love.

Rest, God is Listening

It is no secret what you feel
Or what you are going through.
Your pain and fears are not trapped inside of you
With no escape.
God is always listening,
Waiting for you to place
Your fears and troubles in the palm of His hands…
Waiting for you to trust Him with all of your heart and soul.
He is the producer of peace and contentment.
His love and mercy will never abandon you.
Rest, God is listening…
Trust and you will be heard.

Soothing

The thought of you
Soothes every corner of my mind.
Soothing, is your smile that sprinkles
Warm joy all over my soul…
Soothing, is your hand in mine
On a walk after the sun has gone home.
Soothing is your voice-
The first and last velvety tune I hear of the day.
Soothing is in the comforting words you say.
With your love and understanding-
You always seem to move me…
That is why your love in my life is
Very, very soothing….

Clear View

I see tomorrow as a day where
Miracles await discovery and lessons are to be learned.
Crystal clear is the story I have to tell of joy
And sorrow-
Combined I have a balanced life of trials and triumph.
One without the other,
I have an unrealistic view of life.
Clearly, I see what lies ahead.
Even through hazy horizons;
I will continue to move on-
Knowing that my determination
Has the power to remove clouds
Before they try to settle
And obstruct my lucent view.

Can't Explain

Forever can not begin to measure how long
My love will thrive for you.
Love alone could never unveil the feeling my heart
Dedicates to you.
Laughter could never mimic the bliss I feel when I am with you.
Having you to love is so dynamic and beautiful…
Yet it remains an incredible phenomenon
That words can never explain.

Ingredients

One cup of your love mixed into my soul,
Is enough happiness to finish my mold.

One dash of your sugar melts right in,
Just the right amount of sweetness-
For our hearts to blend.

A teaspoon of your strength
Goes a long way-
To uplift my spirits on trying days.

Let's not forget this recipe that we
Created together…

Ingredients of true love-
Relished forever.

Needle and Thread

I have the needle.
You have the thread.
At times I may lack a few
Of my tools.
Will you lend me a couple of spools?
When I am down, I need your smile.
I may even need your ear for a while.
When I am happy join in my glee.
Your genuine interest means the world to me.
When I feel alone I may need your hand,
Guide me to your heart where I will find a friend.
Together we will sew away loose ends…
I have the needle.
You have the thread.
We will always stitch our hearts with trust.
I have the needle.
You have the thread…
Together we will wear a garment of love.

In Motion

The path was a worn circle of regret,
Unpromising it led;
But familiar it was yet.
Fixed pavement once led the way instead-
Never realizing the dead end lying ahead.
The road you walk is a road in motion…
As long as you try, you are moving towards something.
Destroyed is the asphalt where you patterned steps
To repeat mistakes wrapped in regret.
The detour points to a brand new road,
Bearing no footprints of the lost without hope.
The road you walk is a road in motion…
As long as you try, you are moving towards something.
No longer afraid to pound new ground-
Your direction is set and you are turned around.
Honor is in the freedom of your footpath.
You carved it with determination and prepared it to last.
The road you walk is a road in motion…
As long as you try, you are moving towards something.

Spanish Shores

The hush of peace surrounds you.
Transparent blue waters call you by name.
Lucid sunshine engulfs your body;
As you bathe in joy on Spanish shores.
Warm white sand between your toes,
Creating a texture that is well known.
A bathing suit and a cozy spot to witness
The art that no man owns.
In awe you capture the aqua blue bay
Displaying a ray of brilliance.
The sun is a canvas of blended yellows
Leaving a rich balmy feeling.
You find a new wonder to marvel.
There is more beauty than ever before-
And only to be expected;
When you laze in a place called Spanish shores.

Art of A Woman

A smile that says many things;
I love you, I understand, or
You make me happy.
Gestures to get her point across-
Pouting lips, crossed arms,
Or raised brows.
Soft skin like the petals of a rose.
A walk that demands attention.
Strength that holds a baby on one hip,
And a grocery bag on the other.
A body that is physically fit even after the
Kids have arrived.
A gift to her man, not a possession.
A best friend to herself and a
Blessing to others.
Virtuous, proud, intelligent;
All an art of being a woman.

Art of A True Man

Not afraid to express his feelings
Or shed tears of emotion.
Knowing how to charm
With his intellect and smile.
Responsible with a direction in his path.
A proud example in his child's eyes.
Hard working-
But knows the definition of quality time.
A strength that radiates confidence.
A heart that is not afraid
To be loved, or to give love.
A friend to his wife;
Yet in tune with his own being.
The art of a true man knows
When to set aside control
And let God finish the job…

Speak To Me

I feel Your warm breath around me on a summer day.
Thunderstorms rumble when You have something to say.
I see Your smile sitting in the bright blue clouds.
I hear the wind hush by in a gentle breeze…
Lord, I hear what You are saying
When You speak to me.

Reasons

You are the reason that smiling is a joy.
You are the reason that sunsets warm my heart.
You are the reason that beautiful things remind me of you.
You are the reason why my heart beats,
My soul sings,
And my love has a place to go.

Single Mom

Love was supposed to last forever…
You are alone with your child making a way.
No one told you that there would be days,
When the struggle felt worse than the gain…
But you held on to your faith single mom.

Days when food looked scarce on the table,
You worked your way through school anyway.
You held on to your faith single mom.

Juggling a career and a child on your own.
At times you felt down and alone.
You still kneeled and praised God's holy name.
You held on to your faith single mom.

When the bills were piled up and the baby was sick.
You prayed twice as hard, refusing to quit.
You thanked God for blessing you through the day.
You held on to your faith single mom.

Lyrics of the Soul

Many trials you made it through.
Now you have testaments to share of truth,
Of how the Lord's love provided for you.
In the Lord you knew to store your faith.
There were times you had to be patient and wait…
But you held on to your faith single mom.

Perfect Life

The Lord is interested in perfecting your life.
There is no greater love than what He can provide.
You are the apple of His eye,
His dying for you is proof.
He had your purpose defined before you entered the womb.
Happiness and prosperity is His goal for you and I.
It comes with a price that the soul must buy.
Trust, faith, and prayer is what it will cost.
His perfect love will lift you if your spirit falls.
Through the Lord all things are possible…
Even to the blindest eye.
The Lord will show you blessings
Your tongue won't deny.
You will prosper and reach the greatest heights,
Trust the Lord-
He is there to perfect your life.

Autobiography

I began writing short stories at age nine to entertain the children in my old neighborhood of Detroit, Michigan, where I was born and raised for eleven years. I moved to Dallas, Texas at age twelve and by fourteen, my poetry evolved and had taken on a more amplifying approach. Yesterday, Today, Tomorrow was the first self-encouraging poem that I had ever written. The poem went from pages of my personal journal and stayed with me throughout life. I felt motivated to write inspirational poetry to express the spiritual blessings in life, and to encourage others with words of faith and love. I have always felt compelled to reach people and touch them in the core of their hearts; being the hopeless romantic and empathetic soul that I am. The need to express the beauty in life that is full of Christ's love and the desire to encourage others, is the driving force behind my dream of being a poet today.

Printed in the United States
88892LV00004B/328-345/A